Who Said That?

Everyday sayings with roots in the Bible!

Shari S. Abbott

Who Said That?

Everyday sayings with roots in the Bible!

That I may publish with the voice of thanksgiving, and tell of all thy wondrous works. (Psalm 26:7)

Published by Psalm267 Publishing
www.psalm267.com

Printed in the United States of America

ISBN: 978-0-9885513-3-6

Dedicated to the Word of God
*and the God of the Word**

Thy word have I hid in mine heart. Psalm 119:11

I will not forget thy word. Psalm 119:16

I trust in thy word. Psalm 119:42

Thy word is my comfort in my affliction. Psalm 119:50

Be merciful unto me according to thy word. Psalm 119:58

I hope in thy word. Psalm 119:81, 114

Uphold me according unto thy word. Psalm 119:116

Order my steps in thy word. Psalm 119:133

Thy word is very pure. Psalm 119:140

My heart standeth in awe of thy word. Psalm 119:161

I rejoice at thy word. Psalm 119:162

Give me understanding according to thy word. Psalm 119:169

Deliver me according to thy word. Psalm 119:170

My tongue shall speak of thy word. Psalm 119:172

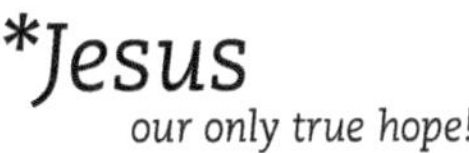

for the word of God
is quick, and powerful...

(Hebrews 4:12)

Contents

Who Said That?

Everyday sayings with roots in the Bible

Shari S. Abbott

Psalm267 Publishing

*That I may publish with the voice of thanksgiving,
and tell of all thy wondrous works.* (Psalm 26:7)

If anyone speaks,
he should do it as
one speaking the
very words of God.
(1 Peter 4:11, NIV)

FOREWORD

We hear many negative reports these days, documenting the state of our nation and the breakdown of culture. So when something encouraging comes along we like to, "'spread the news." Such is the case with the ministry and writings of Shari Abbott. A few years ago as I read Shari's first book and began to learn of her ministry, I was not only impressed but also deeply encouraged.

Shari Abbott brings to the table not only biblical knowledge and skill as a communicator, but also years of experience from her career in the professional world. Today she is successfully helping people through some of life's valleys with a message of truth and hope that all need to hear.

I believe God has positioned Shari for perhaps her most fruitful endeavor yet: Release of the book *Who Said That? Everyday sayings with roots in the Bible.* Let me explain why a book like this is needed at this time.

Current statistics about knowledge of God's truth is troubling. How much do Americans (church members included) know about the most important book in history, the Bible?

Researcher and scholar George Barna reports:

- Fewer than half of all adults can name the four Gospels.
- 60 percent of Americans cannot name even five of the Ten Commandments.
- 82 percent of Americans believe "God helps those who help themselves" is a Bible verse.
- 12 percent of adults believe that Joan of Arc was Noah's wife.
- Four out of ten Americans believe that when Jesus Christ was on earth He committed sins.
- Five out of ten believe that anyone who is generally good or does enough good things for others during their life will earn a place in Heaven.
- Only one out of ten Christians base their moral decision-making on the principles taught in the Bible.

These statistics graphically reveal that our nation is more uninformed about the content of the Bible than ever. But they also illustrate the need for great resources like Shari Abbott's new book. She has created a tool that is equipping churches and individuals to know not only treasures from the Bible (common, everyday sayings), but also the simple path to having a relationship with God Himself (see "Yada, Yada, Yada" and "A Three Strand Cord," pages 73-77).

Our nation urgently needs to hear the good news of salvation today. Perhaps even you, reading this right now, need clarification about where you stand with God. Would you like to be at peace with God? Wouldn't it be great to have assurance and real certainty about one's relationship with Christ? Wouldn't it be encouraging to be confident and well-equipped in helping others with spiritual needs?

If these questions stir your heart, then this book is for you! People need all the help they can get in navigating the murky waters of a culture that no longer affirms truth or morality. I applaud the work of my trusted colleague, Shari Abbott, and I highly recommend her research and ministry.

Now, enjoy the everyday sayings...from the Bible!

Alex McFarland

Alex McFarland
director, Apologetics and Christian Worldview
North Greenville University, SC
www.alexmcfarland.com

Let your speech be always with grace, that you may know how you ought to answer every man.

(Colossians 4:6)

INTRODUCTION

Words are important! Whether spoken or written, words remain our primary means of communication in human relationships. Gestures, facial expressions, and drawings can never replace words. Nothing can communicate as clearly as a few spoken or written words.

Throughout the centuries, short phrases and sayings have become popular for expressing thoughts and emotions. Many of these sayings convey their meanings using figurative language, while others have literal meaning. However popular they might be, most of them are spoken without any thought to where they came from or how they originated.

Perhaps you grew up hearing sayings like "fight the good fight," "you're the apple of my eye," or "there's nothing new under the sun." You might even incorporate some of them into your everyday conversations.

Have you ever wondered where those sayings came from? Most people are unaware that many of these common, everyday sayings derive from the words of the Bible, dating back thousands of years.

The English Translations of the Bible

John Wycliffe, a 14th-century Oxford professor, scholar, theologian, and lay preacher, was the first person to translate the Christian Scriptures into English. It is believed that Wycliffe personally translated the Gospels of Matthew, Mark,

Luke, and John, and possibly the entire New Testament, while his associates translated the Old Testament. Wycliffe translated from the only source available to him at the time, the Latin Vulgate, and completed his work by 1384, predating the printing press. Wycliffe produced dozens of manuscript copies of the Bible.

In the 1450s, Johannes Gutenberg invented the printing press. Notably, the first book ever printed was a Bible (in the Latin language).

In 1525, William Tyndale, an English contemporary of Martin Luther, translated the New Testament. Tyndale's translation was the first printed Bible in English.

In 1535, Myles Coverdale finished translating and then printed the first complete Bible in the English language.

John Rogers printed the second complete English Bible in 1537 under the pseudonym of Thomas Matthew (a name that Tyndale had used at one time). This Bible contained portions from Tyndale's and Coverdale's translations, as well as some of Roger's own translations. It was most commonly known as the Matthew-Tyndale Bible.

At King Henry VIII's request, the Archbishop of Canterbury Thomas Cranmer hired Myles Coverdale in 1539 to publish the Great Bible. It became the first English Bible authorized for public use and distributed to churches. It was known as the Great Bible because of its large size. Between April 1539 and December 1541, seven editions of this Bible were printed.

In 1560, the Geneva Bible was printed. Another complete English Bible, this version was the first Bible to number the verses in each book. Chapters also had extensive marginal notes and references, making this the first English Bible considered a Study Bible. Shakespeare, in his plays, quoted extensively from the Geneva Bible, and it quickly became the choice of English speaking Christians for more than 100 years. The Geneva Bible was used by both the Puritans and the Pilgrims, and it is often referred to as the "Bible of the Protestant Reformation."

From 1604-1609, about 50 scholars embarked on a new translation. It went to press in 1610, and the first editions were available in 1611. The Bible was titled in old English as, "THE HOLY BIBLE, Conteyning [Containing] the Old Testament, and the New: Newly Translated out of the Originall Tongues: and with the former Translations diligently compared and reuised [revised], by his Majesties speciall Commandment. Appointed to be read in Churches."

This Bible came to be commonly known as the Authorized Version (AV) or the King James Bible (KJB). From the words of the 1611 King James Bible, we can find the origins of the common, every- day sayings contained in this book.

Each is a short, pithy saying that derives from the

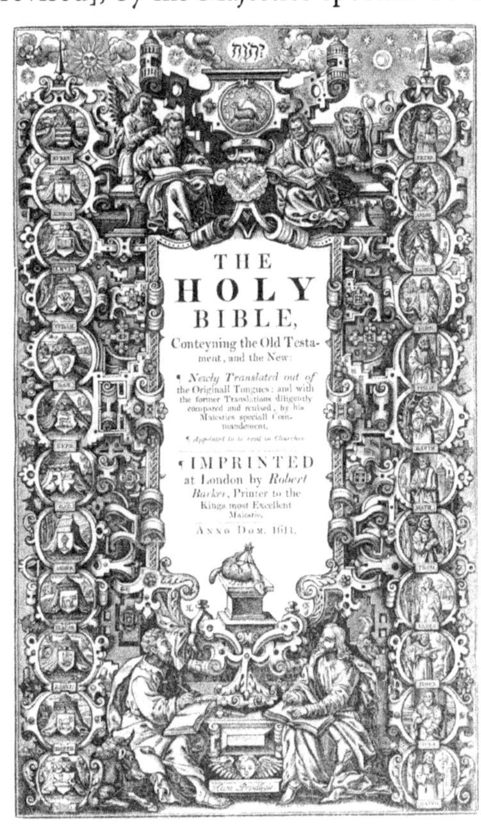

THE
HOLY
BIBLE,
Conteyning the Old Testament, and the New:
Newly Translated out of the Originall Tongues: and with the former Translations diligently compared and reuised, by his Maiesties speciall Commandement.
Appointed to be read in Churches.
IMPRINTED
at London by Robert Barker, Printer to the Kings most Excellent Maiestie.
Anno Dom. 1611.

wisdom of Holy Scripture and has stood the test of time.

As Christians, we understand that the Word of God is the instruction manual for everyday living. Therefore, it should be no wonder to us that these popular sayings originated from God's Word.

We should always remember that words are important. They can easily be given away, but can never be taken back. They influence our interactions with others and either promote the growth of relationships or bring about their demise.

We encourage you to speak precisely and with intent. Choose your words carefully. And when using common, everyday sayings, be certain that you understand their meaning and apply them correctly.

Although this book presents and explains many common, everyday sayings derived from the Bible, I'm certain there are more. I challenge you to come up with other sayings with biblical origins. If you do, please email them to us at hope@reasonsforhopeJesus.com.

Now, let's take a look at

everyday sayings. . .

from the Bible!

Everyday sayings with roots in the Bible!

A drop in the bucket.

A very small thing; a very small portion of a much larger whole.

Isaiah 40:15 Behold, the nations are as a drop of a bucket, and are counted as the small dust of the balance: behold, he taketh up the isles as a very little thing.

A fly in the ointment.

A reference to something very small, but capable of spoiling the whole.

Ecclesiastes 10:1 Dead flies cause the ointment of the apothecary to send forth a stinking savour:

Aha!

An exclamation of surprise or grief.

Psalm 35:21 Yea, they opened their mouth wide against me, and said, Aha, aha, our eye hath seen it.

Psalm 40:15 Let them be desolate for a reward of their shame that say unto me, Aha, aha.

Ezekiel 25:3 And say unto the Ammonites, Hear the word of the Lord GOD; Thus saith the Lord GOD; Because thou saidst, Aha, against my sanctuary, when it was profaned; and against the land of Israel, when it was desolate; and against the house of Judah, when they went into captivity;

A heart of stone.

A hard heart. A heart untouched, unmoved, uncaring, or unfeeling.

1 Samuel 25:37 But it came to pass in the morning, when the wine was gone out of Nabal, and his wife had told him these things, that his heart died within him, and he became as a stone.

Job 41:24 His heart is as firm as a stone; yea, as hard as a piece of the nether millstone .

A horse of a different color.

Someone or something completely different than the rest and noticeably so.

Zechariah 1:8 I saw by night, and behold a man riding upon a red horse, and he stood among the myrtle trees that were in the bottom; and behind him were there red horses, speckled, and white.

A house divided cannot stand.

When a structure is divided/broken it will be weakened to a point that it falls/fails.

Matthew 12:25 And Jesus knew their thoughts, and said unto them, Every kingdom divided against itself is brought to desolation; and every city or house divided against itself shall not stand:

Mark 3:25 And if a house be divided against itself, that house cannot stand.

Luke 11:17 But he, knowing their thoughts, said unto them, Every kingdom divided against itself is brought to desolation; and a house divided against a house falleth.

The expression "a house divided" was used by Abraham Lincoln in an address prior to his presidency on June 16, 1858. In that address, which came to be knows as "A House Divided Speech," Lincoln said:

> *A house divided against itself cannot stand. I believe this government cannot endure, permanently, half slave and half free. I do not expect the Union to be dissolved — I do not expect the house to fall — but I do expect it will cease to be divided. It will become all one thing or all the other. Either the opponents of slavery will arrest the further spread of it, and place it where the public mind shall rest in the belief that it is in the course of ultimate extinction; or its advocates will push it forward, till it shall become lawful in all the States, old as well as new — North as well as South.*[1]

A lamb to the slaughter.

Someone unconcerned or unaware of an impending disaster or catastrophe -- just as a lamb is unaware when it is taken to be slaughtered.

Jeremiah 11:19 But I was like a lamb or an ox that is brought to the slaughter...

Isaiah 53:7 He was oppressed, and he was afflicted, yet he opened not his mouth: he is brought as a lamb to the slaughter...

1 "A House Divided," Info USA, Us Department of State, http://usinfo.org/enus/government/overview/22.html

Act 8:32 1161 The place of the scripture which he read was this, He was led as a sheep to the slaughter; and like a lamb dumb before his shearer, so opened he not his mouth:

A law unto themselves.

People who do things their own way and follow their own rules and ideas rather than following more universally accepted procedures or agreeing with the ideas of the majority.

Romans 2:14 For when the Gentiles, which have not the law, do by nature the things contained in the law, these, having not the law, are a law unto themselves:

A little bird told me.

To be told by a private or secret source. Often used to indicate that the source will not be revealed.

Ecclesiastes 10:20 Curse not the king, no not in thy thought; and curse not the rich in thy bedchamber: for a bird of the air shall carry the voice, and that which hath wings shall tell the matter.

The idea of a bird carrying a message is also found in the post-flood account recorded in Genesis 8.

All in all.

Completely. Entirely. Taking all things into consideration.

1 Corinthians 12:6 And there are diversities of operations, but it is the same God which worketh all in all.

1 Corinthians 15:28 And when all things shall be subdued unto him, then shall the Son also himself be subject unto him that put all things under him, that God may be all in all.

Ephesians 1:23 ...the fullness of him [Jesus] that filleth all in all.

All things to all men.

Pleasing to everyone, or meeting the needs of all.

1 Corinthians 9:22 To the weak became I as weak, that I might gain the weak: I am made All things to all men, that I might by all means save some.

All things must pass.

Things determined to happen will eventually come about.

Matthew 24:6 And ye shall hear of wars and rumours of wars: see that ye be not troubled: for all these things must come to pass, but the end is not yet.

A man after my own heart.

A kindred spirit - someone with whom I agree.

1 Samuel 13:14 But now thy kingdom shall not continue: the LORD hath sought him a man after his own heart, and the LORD hath commanded him to be captain over his people...

Am I my brother's keeper?

Literal meaning: To be one's guardian or protector.

Genesis 4:9 And the LORD said unto Cain, Where is Abel thy brother? And he said, I know not: Am I my brother's keeper?

A prophet has no honor in his own home.

An expression that is used of someone who is highly regarded by many, but whose family and close friends will not consider, or take seriously, their words or works.

John 4:44 For Jesus himself testified, that a prophet hath no honour in his own country.

Apple of my eye.

The literal meaning is the central aperture of the eye. Figuratively it refers to something of great importance to you, or most often to *someone* you cherish above all others.

Deuteronomy 32:10 He found him in a desert land, and in the waste howling wilderness; he led him about, he instructed him, he kept him as the apple of his eye.

Zechariah 2:8 For thus saith the LORD of hosts; After the glory hath he sent me unto the nations which spoiled you: for he that toucheth you toucheth the apple of his eye.

A scapegoat.

A person upon whom blame is laid; someone who suffers the consequences of another's actions.

Leviticus 16:9-10 And Aaron shall bring the goat upon which the LORD'S lot fell, and offer him for a sin offering. But the goat, on which the lot fell to be the scapegoat, shall be presented alive before the LORD, to make an atonement with him, and to let him go for a scapegoat into the wilderness.

As old as Methuselah.

A reference to being very old.

Genesis 5:27 And all the days of Methuselah were nine hundred sixty and nine years: and he died.

As old as the hills.

Exceedingly old.

Job 15:7 Art thou the first man that was born? or wast thou made before the hills?

As white as snow.

Pure white.

Numbers 12:10 And the cloud departed from off the tabernacle; and, behold, Miriam became leprous, white as snow: and Aaron looked upon Miriam, and, behold, she was leprous.

Isaiah 1:18 Come now, and let us reason together, saith the LORD: though your sins be as scarlet, they shall be as white as snow; though they be red like crimson, they shall be as wool.

Matthew 28:3 His countenance was like lightning, and his raiment white as snow:

Revelation 1:14 His head and his hairs were white like wool, as white as snow; and his eyes were as a flame of fire;

As you sow, so shall you reap.

The kind of deeds you perform, good or bad, will determine the kind of response you will receive. What you say and do has consequences.

Galatians 6:7 Be not deceived; God is not mocked: for whatsoever a man soweth, that shall he also reap.

A sharp tongue.

A tongue that speaks cutting words.

Psalm 52:2 Thy tongue deviseth mischiefs; like a sharp razor, working deceitfully .

Psalm 57:4 My soul is among lions: and I lie even among them that are set on fire, even the sons of men, whose teeth are spears and arrows, and their tongue a sharp sword.

Ashes to ashes, dust to dust.

This literally means that we come from dust and our bodies will return to dust. Figuratively it means that everything returns to what it began as.

Ecclesiastes 3:20 All go unto one place; all are of the dust, and all turn to dust again.

A time to be born and a time to die. A time and a place for everything.

There is an appointed time for everything.

Ecclesiastes 3:1-2 To every thing there is a season, and a time to every purpose under the heaven: A time to be born, and a time to die; a time to plant, and a time to pluck up that which is planted.

At my wit's end.

At the limit of one's mental resources. At a complete loss, unable to think of what to do. At the point of no return.

Psalm 107:27 They reel to and fro, and stagger like a drunken man, and are at their wit's end.

A wolf in sheep's clothing.

A deception of presenting oneself as good, gentle or truthful when in reality evil or malicious intent is being hidden (usually hidden in wait, to attack or be revealed at an unsuspecting time).

Matthew 7:15 Beware of false prophets, which come to you in sheep's clothing, but inwardly they are ravening wolves.

Baptism by fire.

(also Baptism *in* fire or Baptism *with* fire)

A reference to a first experience that is under extremely difficult or trying circumstances. Often in reference to a soldier's first experience in battle.

Matthew 3:11 I indeed baptize you with water unto repentance: but he that cometh after me is mightier than I, whose shoes I am not worthy to bear: he shall baptize you with the Holy Ghost, and with fire

Beat your swords into plowshares.

Putting an end to killing and war, and turning to peaceful pursuits.

In the garden of the United Nations in New York City is a 1959 gift from the old Soviet Union. The sculpture bears the words of Isaiah 2:4 and depicts a man holding a sword and beating it into a plow with a hammer. The sculpture express-

es man's desire to bring about world peace.
Isaiah 2:4 And he shall judge among the nations, and shall rebuke many people: and they shall beat their swords into plowshares, and their spears into pruninghooks: nation shall not lift up sword against nation, neither shall they learn war any more.

Bent out of shape.

This phrase is the modern equivalent of the phrase "pressed out of measure" and means to have been pushed to the limit.

2 Corinthians 1:8 For we would not, brethren, have you ignorant of our trouble which came to us in Asia, that we were pressed out of measure, above strength, insomuch that we despaired even of life.

Bite the dust.

To fall to the ground, wounded or dead; to fall prostrate on the ground.

Psalm 72:9 They that dwell in the wilderness shall bow before him; and his enemies shall lick the dust.

Blinded by the light (see also, I saw the light).

To have your understanding illuminated. From the passage that tells of Paul seeing a great light from heaven and subsequently his conversion to faith in Christ.

Acts 9:3-9 And as he journeyed, he came near Damascus: and

suddenly there shined round about him a light from heaven: And he fell to the earth, and heard a voice saying unto him, Saul, Saul, why persecutest thou me? And he said, Who art thou, Lord? And the Lord said, I am Jesus whom thou persecutest: it is hard for thee to kick against the pricks. And he trembling and astonished said, Lord, what wilt thou have me to do? And the Lord said unto him, Arise, and go into the city, and it shall be told thee what thou must do. And the men which journeyed with him stood speechless, hearing a voice, but seeing no man. And Saul arose from the earth; and when his eyes were opened, he saw no man: but they led him by the hand, and brought him into Damascus. And he was three days without sight, and neither did eat nor drink.

Blood money.

Money paid to someone for providing evidence that will convict another; money paid to next of kin to buy-off his right to seek blood for blood; money paid to someone to betray another, as Judas was paid blood-money.

Matthew 27:6 And the chief priests took the silver pieces, and said, It is not lawful for to put them into the treasury, because it is the price of blood.

Blow your own horn.

To proclaim your accomplishments, usually by bragging and most often with a desire for acknowledgment or personal gain.

Matthew 6:2 Therefore when thou doest thine alms, do not sound a trumpet before thee, as the hypocrites do in the synagogues and in the streets, that they may have glory of men. Verily I say unto you, They have their reward.

Breach of promise.

Legally this means the withdrawal of a marriage proposal or other contract. Biblically it refers to a separation or rejection.

Numbers 14:34 After the number of the days in which ye searched the land, even forty days, each day for a year, shall ye bear your iniquities, even forty years, and ye shall know my breach of promise.

Busybody

Someone who meddles in the affairs of others.

2 Thessalonians 3:11 For we hear that there are some which walk among you disorderly, working not at all, but are busybodies.

By the skin of my teeth.

Usually used in reference to a narrow escape from a disaster.

Job 19:20 My bone cleaveth to my skin and to my flesh, and I am escaped with the skin of my teeth.

By the sweat of your brow.

Accomplishing something by hard work.

Genesis 3:19 "And unto Adam he [God] said, Because thou hast hearkened unto the voice of thy wife, and hast eaten of the tree, of which I commanded thee, saying, Thou shalt not eat of it: cursed is the ground for thy sake; in sorrow shalt thou eat of it all the days of thy life; Thorns also and thistles shall it bring forth to thee; and thou shalt eat the herb of the field; In the sweat of thy face shalt thou eat bread, till thou return unto the ground...

Can a leopard change its spots?

A proverbial question, asking if a person or creature can really change its innate being.

Jeremiah 13:23 Can the Ethiopian change his skin, or the leopard his spots? then may ye also do good, that are accustomed to do evil.

Charity begins at home.

This means that you should take care of family and people close to you before you care for others.

The word charity in the King James 1611 Bible is an English translation of the Greek word agape, which means love, affection, or benevolence. Charity refers to sacrificial love and giving of one's time and resources. So charity should start with family and friends (especially brothers and sisters in the Lord), and then spread to others.

1 Timothy 5:8 But if any provide not for his own, and specially for those of his own house, he hath denied the faith, and is worse than an infidel.

Galatians 6:10 As we have therefore opportunity, let us do good unto all men, especially unto them who are of the household of faith.

Come hell or high water.

This phrase expresses a desire to do something regardless of the consequences. It is often used defiantly, but can be used to express determination in the face of great difficulty.

Although not a direct biblical origin, this phrase certainly alludes to impending catastrophe and judgment. Hell, of course, being final judgment and "high water" being an allusion to judgment by the Great Flood of Noah's time.

Dead dog.

In reference to a person it implies someone who is no longer important, relevant or significant.

1 Samuel 24:14 After whom is the king of Israel come out? after whom dost thou pursue? after a dead dog, after a flea.

2 Samuel 9:8 And he bowed himself, and said, What is thy servant, that thou shouldest look upon such a dead dog as I am?

Do as I say, not as I do.

An excuse by someone saying you should do the right thing, even though they do not.
Matthew 23:2-3 Saying, The scribes and the Pharisees sit in Moses' seat: All therefore whatsoever they bid you observe, that observe and do; but do not ye after their works: for they say, and do not.

Dog returns to its vomit.

This has a meaning of returning to unpleasant things or bad habits or behaviors.

Proverbs 26:11 As a dog returneth to his vomit, so a fool returneth to his folly.

Do unto others as you would have others do unto you. (The Golden Rule)

Treat others as you would like to be treated.

Matthew 7:12 Therefore all things whatsoever ye would that men should do to you, do ye even so to them: for this is the law and the prophets.

Don't borrow trouble.

A warning against creating problems by looking for trouble and expecting it.

Matthew 6:34 Therefore do not worry about tomorrow, for tomorrow will worry about its own things. Sufficient for the day is its own trouble.

Don't cast your pearls before swine.

Don't give items of value or quality to those who do not appreciate them.

Matthew 7:6 Give not that which is holy unto the dogs, neither cast ye your pearls before swine, lest they trample them under their feet, and turn again and rend you.

Don't let the sun go down on your anger.

(Don't go to bed mad.)

Let go of anger before the end of the day, thereby limiting an emotion that can lead to ungodly words or actions.

Ephesians 4:26 Be ye angry, and sin not: let not the sun go down upon your wrath:

Doubting Thomas

A reference to skeptical people who won't believe the word of others, but instead require proof.

John 20: 24-25 But Thomas, one of the twelve, called Didymus, was not with them when Jesus came. The other disciples therefore said unto him, We have seen the Lord. But he said unto them, Except I shall see in his hands the print of the nails, and put my finger into the print of the nails, and thrust my hand into his side, I will not believe.

Eat, drink and be merry.

The literal meaning is to find happiness by indulging in pleasures of food, drink and merriment.

Luke 12:19 And I will say to my soul, Soul, thou hast much goods laid up for many years; take thine ease, eat, drink, and be merry.

Eye for an eye, tooth for a tooth.

The idea that compensation or retaliation should be of equal value.

Exodus 21:24 Eye for eye, tooth for tooth, hand for hand, foot for foot,

Leviticus 24:20 Breach for breach, eye for eye, tooth for tooth: as he hath caused a blemish in a man, so shall it be done to him again.

Deuteronomy 19:21 And thine eye shall not pity; but life shall go for life, eye for eye, tooth for tooth, hand for hand, foot for foot

Matthew 5:38 Ye have heard that it hath been said, An eye for an eye, and a tooth for a tooth:

Faith can move mountains.

Faith powerful and can bring about amazing results.

Matthew 21:21 Jesus answered and said unto them, Verily I say unto you, If ye have faith, and doubt not, ye shall not only do this which is done to the fig tree, but also if ye shall say unto this mountain, Be thou removed, and be thou cast into the sea; it shall be done.

Fall on your sword.

Literally used of someone who brings about their own physical death (by suicide). Figuratively used of a "death" by resignation, failure, etc.

1 Samuel 31:4-5 Then said Saul unto his armourbearer, Draw thy sword, and thrust me through therewith; lest these uncircumcised come and thrust me through, and abuse me. But his armourbearer would not; for he was sore afraid. Therefore Saul took a sword, and fell upon it. And when his armourbearer saw that Saul was dead, he fell likewise upon his sword, and died with him.

Fed up with it.

An expression of frustration in which the limits of tolerance or patience have been exceeded.

Proverbs 1:31 Therefore shall they eat of the fruit of their own way, and be filled with their own devices.

Feet of clay.

A hidden flaw that weakens or denigrates the character of person who otherwise is admired.

The prophet Daniel interpreted King Nebuchadnezzar's

dream of a statue with head of gold, breast and arms of silver, belly and thighs of brass, legs of iron and feet of iron and clay.

Daniel 2:33 His legs of iron, his feet part of iron and part of clay.

Fell on rocky ground.

A reference usually to spoken words that are ignored, unpopular or considered to be of no value.

Matthew 13:5 Some fell upon stony places, where they had not much earth: and forthwith they sprung up, because they had no deepness of earth.

Fight the good fight.

Don't give up on worthwhile efforts. Also, an evangelical call to live godly and to share the gospel.

1 Timothy 6:12 Fight the good fight of faith, lay hold on eternal life, whereunto thou art also called, and hast professed a good profession before many witnesses.

2 Timothy 4:7 I have fought a good fight, I have finished my course, I have kept the faith.

Filthy lucre.

Lucre means gain. Filthy lucre is a reference to deceitful or dishonest gain. This phrase is often used in reference to illegal monetary gain

1 Timothy 3:3 Not given to wine, no striker, not greedy of filthy lucre; but patient, not a brawler, not covetous.

Titus 1:11 Whose mouths must be stopped, who subvert whole houses, teaching things which they ought not, for filthy lucre's sake.

1 Peter 5:2 Feed the flock of God which is among you, taking the oversight thereof, not by constraint, but willingly; not for filthy lucre, but of a ready mind;

For everything there is a season. (There's a season for everything)

There is an appropriate time for everything.

Ecclesiastes 3:1-8 To every thing there is a season, and a time to every purpose under the heaven: A time to be born, and a time to die; a time to plant, and a time to pluck up that which is planted; A time to kill, and a time to heal; a time to break down, and a time to build up; A time to weep, and a time to laugh; a time to mourn, and a time to dance; A time to cast away stones, and a time to gather stones together; a time to embrace, and a time to refrain from embracing; A time to get, and a time to lose; a time to keep, and a time to cast away; A time to rend, and a time to sew; a time to keep silence, and a time to speak; A time to love, and a time to hate; a time of war, and a time of peace.

In the 1950s Pete Seeger wrote the song To Everything There Is A Season, adapting the words of these verses from the book of Ecclesiastes to music. It was recorded and released by The Limeliters on their album Folk Matinee. Shortly thereafter Seeger recorded and released the song entitled

Turn! Turn! Turn! (To Everything There Is A Season) on his album, The Bitter and the Sweet. The song achieved international fame when it was recorded by the American folk rock band The Byrds in 1965, and reached #1 on the Billboard Hot 100 chart and #26 on the UK Singles Chart. The song continues in popularity, having been sung or recorded by numerous artists. The song was featured in the motion picture Forrest Gump. It has also been featured on the small screen, in TV episodes of The Wonder Years, The Simpsons and Cold Case.

From strength to strength.

Increasing power and might.

Psalm 84:7 They go from strength to strength, every one of them in Zion appeareth before God.

Give a man enough rope and he'll hang himself.

From the story of Haman in the Book of Esther, this phrase refers to a reversal of events leading to one's demise. In Esther, Haman plotted to completely annihilate the Jews. As his plot unraveled his evil intent was revealed and he was hanged.

Esther 7:10 So they hanged Haman on the gallows that he had prepared for Mordecai. Then was the king's wrath pacified.

Godspeed to you.

To bid someone Godspeed means to express a hope that God will bless and prosper them. The word "speed" means to be cheerful, calmly happy or well off. We find a warning in the Bible to not wish Godspeed upon those who do not know God.

2 John 1:9-10 Whosoever transgresseth, and abideth not in the doctrine of Christ, hath not God. He that abideth in the doctrine of Christ, he hath both the Father and the Son. If there come any unto you, and bring not this doctrine, receive him not into your house, neither bid him God speed.

Go through fire and water.

To experience difficulties or face challenges to gain something or to emerge stronger.

Numbers 31:23 Every thing that may abide the fire, ye shall make it go through the fire, and it shall be clean: nevertheless it shall be purified with the water of separation: and all that abideth not the fire ye shall make go through the water.

Going the extra mile.

Going above and beyond that which is expected or that which is called for.

Matthew 5:41 And whosoever shall compel thee to go a mile, go with him twain [two].

Going to hell in a hand basket.

This phrase refers to someone who has given-in to the evils of the world and is headed for judgment.

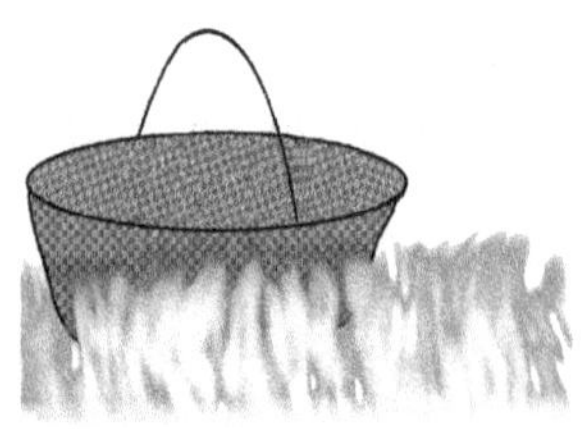

The phrase comes from the vision given to the prophet Zechariah, recorded in Zechariah 5:5-11. A woman (defined as wickedness) is in a ephah (basket). The basket is being lowered by two more women (also wicked) with wings of a stork (defined by God as an unclean bird in Leviticus 11:13-19). Shinar is another name for Babylon (an ungodly, wicked kingdom). This basket is being carried to a place of wickedness and "shall be established" (it will remain there) "upon her own base" (the foundation of wickedness).

Zechariah 5:5-11 Then the angel that talked with me went forth, and said unto me, Lift up now thine eyes, and see what is this that goeth forth. And I said, What is it? And he said, This is an ephah [basket] that goeth forth. He said moreover, This is their resemblance through all the earth. And, behold, there was lifted up a talent of lead: and this is a woman that sitteth in the midst of the ephah. And he said, This is wickedness. And he cast it into the midst of the ephah; and he cast the weight of lead upon the mouth thereof. Then lifted I up mine eyes, and looked, and, behold, there came out two women, and the wind was in their wings; for they had wings like the wings of a stork: and they lifted up the ephah between the earth and the heaven. Then said I to the angel that talked with me, Whither do these bear the ephah? And he said unto me, To build it an house in the land of Shinar: and it shall be established, and set there upon her own base.

He's a good Samaritan.

A reference to a person of compassion who helps others with no expectation of reward.

Luke 10:30-34 And Jesus answering said, A certain man went down from Jerusalem to Jericho, and fell among thieves, which stripped him of his raiment, and wounded him, and departed, leaving him half dead. And by chance there came down a certain priest that way: and when he saw him, he passed by on the other side. And likewise a Levite, when he was at the place, came and looked on him, and passed by on the other side. But a certain Samaritan, as he journeyed, came where he was: and when he saw him, he had compassion on him, And went to him, and bound up his wounds, pouring in oil and wine, and set him on his own beast, and brought him to an inn, and took care of him.

He's the salt of the earth.

Salt is used to make things taste better. It brings out the flavor of food and can also be used to preserve food. In referring to a person this phrase refers to a person of great character, someone who is admired for kind words and good deeds.

Matthew 5:13 Ye are the salt of the earth: but if the salt have lost his savour, wherewith shall it be salted? it is thenceforth good for nothing, but to be cast out, and to be trodden under foot of men.

He gave up the ghost.

The literal meaning is to die.

Genesis 25:8 Then Abraham gave up the ghost, and died in a good old age, an old man, and full of years; and was gathered to his people.

John 19:30 When Jesus therefore had received the vinegar, he said, It is finished: and he bowed his head, and gave up the ghost.

High hand.

A raised (held high) hand signifies acting with authority, determination and confidence.

Exodus 14:8 And the LORD hardened the heart of Pharaoh king of Egypt, and he pursued after the children of Israel: and the children of Israel went out with an high hand.

Numbers 33:3 And they departed from Rameses in the first month, on the fifteenth day of the first month; on the morrow after the passover the children of Israel went out with an high hand in the sight of all the Egyptians.

Hold your tongue.

To stop speaking or to say nothing.

Esther 7:4 For we are sold, I and my people, to be destroyed, to be slain, and to perish. But if we had been sold for bondmen and bondwomen, I had held my tongue, although the enemy could not countervail the king's damage.

Hope against hope.

To continue to desire, believe and trust, even when there are enormous odds against obtaining the desired results.

Romans 4:18 Who against hope believed in hope, that he might become the father of many nations, according to that which was spoken, So shall thy seed be.

In the blink of an eye.

A reference to something happening in an instant.

1 Corinthians 15:52 In a moment, in the twinkling of an eye, at the last trump: for the trumpet shall sound, and the dead shall be raised incorruptible, and we shall be changed.

I'll have his head on a platter.

An expression of anger and hate toward another, accompanied with a desire for the person's demise.

Matthew 14:6-8 But when Herod's birthday was kept, the daughter of Herodias danced before them, and pleased Herod. Whereupon he promised with an oath to give her whatsoever she would ask. And she, being before instructed of her mother, said, Give me here John Baptist's head in a charger [platter].

I'll pin him to the wall.

Indicates an aggressive desire to conquer, or to have control over another.

1 Samuel 18:10-11 ... there was a javelin in Saul's hand. And Saul cast the javelin; for he said, I will smite David even to the wall with it.

In deep water.

In a situation of distress or trouble.

Proverbs 20:5 Counsel in the heart of man is like deep water; but a man of understanding will draw it out.

I saw the light.

(see also, Blinded by the light)

To become aware of something, especially truth. From the passage that tells of Paul seeing a great light from heaven and his subsequent conversion to faith in Christ.

Acts 9:3-6 And as he journeyed, he came near Damascus: and suddenly there shined round about him a light from heaven: And he fell to the earth, and heard a voice saying unto him, Saul, Saul, why persecutest thou me? And he said, Who art thou, Lord? And the Lord said, I am Jesus whom thou persecutest: it is hard for thee to kick against the pricks. And he trembling and astonished said, Lord, what wilt thou have me to do? And the Lord said unto him, Arise, and go into the city, and it shall be told thee what thou must do.

It's better to give than to receive.

A warning against being self-serving or greedy; An understanding that there is joy in doing for others.

Act 20:35 I have shewed you all things, how that so labouring ye ought to support the weak, and to remember the words of the Lord Jesus, how he said, It is more blessed to give than to receive.

I wash my hands of it.

A reference to not accepting responsibility for an action or policy; a complete rejection of any further involvement.

Matthew 27:24 When Pilate saw that he was getting nowhere, but that instead an uproar was starting, he took water and washed his hands in front of the crowd. "I am innocent of this man's blood," he said. "It is your responsibility!"

Labor of love.

Doing work (labor) with a willing and generous spirit.

1 Thessalonians 1:3 We give thanks to God always for you all, making mention of you in our prayers; remembering without ceasing your work of faith, and labour of love, and patience of hope in our Lord Jesus Christ, in the sight of God and our Father

Hebrews 6:10 For God is not unrighteous to forget your work and labour of love, which ye have shewed toward his name, in that ye have ministered to the saints, and do minister.

Laughter is the best medicine.

Medical science says that laughter produces chemicals in our bodies that relieve stress and enhance one's physical and mental health. The Bible told of this long before man's findings.

Proverbs 17:22 A merry heart doeth good like a medicine: but a broken spirit drieth the bones.

Note that the Bible proclaims laughter a good medicine, but not the best medicine. A good cry is actually better than a hearty laugh.

Ecclesiastes 7:3 Sorrow is better than laughter: for by the sadness of the countenance the heart is made better.

Like mother, like daughter. (Similar: "like father, like son" and "the apple doesn't fall far from the tree.")

This implies that the behavior and beliefs of a mother will be reflected in her daughter.

Ezekiel 16:44 Behold, every one that useth proverbs shall use this proverb against thee, saying, As is the mother, so is her daughter.

Like putty in my hand.

This saying often has a negative connotation, because the "putty" is easily molded by another. However, the molding of a person done by God is a gift and a good thing.

Jeremiah 18:6 O house of Israel, cannot I do with you as this potter? saith the LORD. Behold, as the clay is in the potter's hand, so are ye in mine hand, O house of Israel. Live by the sword, die by the sword.

Live by the sword, die by the sword.

If you use violence against others, you can expect violence to be used against you. A life of violence is a two-way street.

Matthew 26:52 Then said Jesus unto him, Put up again thy sword into his place: for all they that take the sword shall perish with the sword.

Living off the fat of the land.

Living on abundant resources.

Genesis 27:39 And Isaac his father answered and said unto him, Behold, thy dwelling shall be the fatness of the earth, and of the dew of heaven from above.

Genesis 45:17-18 And Pharaoh said unto Joseph, Say unto thy brethren, This do ye; lade your beasts, and go, get you unto the land of Canaan; And take your father and your households, and come unto me: and I will give you the good of the land of Egypt, and ye shall eat the fat of the land.

Love of money is the root of all evil.

This has a literal meaning that declares a great truth. Desire for money creates an affection (love for it) that will overtake a person (grow from the root), resulting in evil. This is often misquoted as "*money* is the root of all evil."

1 Timothy 6:10 For the love of money is the root of all evil:

Man does not live by bread alone.

Physical nourishment alone is not sufficient. Man is also a spiritual being and those needs must also be fed.

Matthew 4:4 But he answered and said, It is written, Man shall not live by bread alone, but by every word that proceedeth out of the mouth of God.

Luke 4:4 And Jesus answered him, saying, It is written, That man shall not live by bread alone, but by every word of God.

Many are called, but few are chosen.

This has a literal meaning that from a large calling only a small number are selected.

Matthew 22:11-14 And when the king came in to see the guests, he saw there a man which had not on a wedding garment: And he saith unto him, Friend, how camest thou in hither not having a wedding garment? And he was speechless. Then said the king to the servants, Bind him hand and foot, and take him away, and cast him into outer darkness; there shall be weeping and gnashing of teeth. For many are called, but few are chosen

My cup runneth over.

My needs are satisfied to an extent of overflowing.

Psalm 23:5 Thou preparest a table before me in the presence of mine enemies: thou anointest my head with oil; my cup runneth over.

My right hand man.

A person given authority and honor; a most trusted advisor who is always close at hand. To be at someone's right hand is a good and rewarding position.

The name Benjamin (Genesis 35:18) means son of my right hand. It come from the Hebrew word "ben" meaning son and "yamiyn" meaning the right hand or side of a person, object or locale.

Psalm 16:11 Thou wilt show me the path of life: in thy presence is fullness of joy; at thy right hand there are pleasures for evermore.

Psalm 80:17 Let thy hand be upon the man of thy right hand, upon the son of man whom thou madest strong for thyself.

Isaiah 41:10 Fear thou not; for I am with thee: be not dismayed; for I am thy God: I will strengthen thee; yea, I will help thee; yea, I will uphold thee with the right hand of my righteousness.

Acts 7:55 But he [Stephen], being full of the Holy Ghost, looked up stedfastly into heaven, and saw the glory of God, and Jesus standing on the right hand of God.

Hebrews 12:2 Looking unto Jesus the author and finisher of our faith; who for the joy that was set before him endured the cross, despising the shame, and is set down at the right hand of the throne of God.

No rest for the wicked.

This has a literal meaning that the wicked will not find peace or that they will be tormented.

Isaiah 57:20-21 But the wicked are like the troubled sea, when it cannot rest, whose waters cast up mire and dirt. There is no peace, saith my God, to the wicked.

Nothing but skin and bones.

A reference to a person who is severely underweight, weakened or declining in life.

Job 19:19-20 All my intimate friends detest me; those I love have turned against me. I am nothing but skin and bones Job 19:19-20

Oh, how the mighty have fallen.

An exclamation that the powerful have now been reduced or defeated.

2 Samuel 1:19 The beauty of Israel is slain upon thy high places: how are the mighty fallen!

2 Samuel 1:25 How are the mighty fallen in the midst of the battle!

2 Samuel 1:27 How are the mighty fallen, and the weapons of war perished!

Oh, ye of little faith.

Used in reference to a skeptic, someone with great doubt or unbelief. Christ spoke this as a rebuke to his disciples when they were fearful and when they were not trusting in God's provision for them. This phrase is often used as a humorous jibe directed at someone expressing doubt.

Matthew 8:26 And he saith unto them, Why are ye fearful, O ye of little faith?

Matthew 16:8 Which when Jesus perceived, he said unto them, O ye of little faith, why reason ye among yourselves, because ye have brought no bread? shall he not much more clothe you, O ye of little faith?

Luke 12:28 If then God so clothe the grass, which is to day in the field, and to morrow is cast into the oven; how much more will he clothe you, O ye of little faith?

Old wives' tale.

A reference to folklore stories and superstitions handed down through generations. They are often considered to be something of questionable truth or value.

1 Timothy 4:7 Have nothing to do with godless myths and old wives' tales; rather, train yourself to be godly.

On the one hand.

A phrase used to present two different views, thoughts, ideas, etc. This is often paired with "on the other hand" when presenting both views.

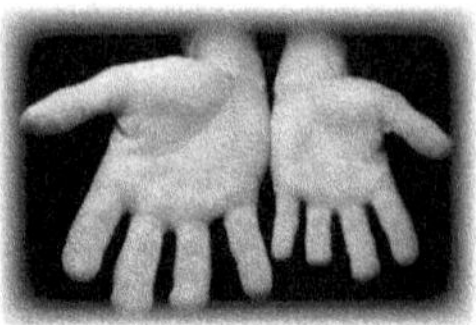

2 Chronicles 3:17 And he reared up the pillars before the temple, one on the right hand, and the other on the left; and called the name of that on the right hand Jachin, and the name of that on the left Boaz. Jachin: that is, He shall establish Boaz: that is, In it is strength

Nehemiah 4:17 They which builded on the wall, and they that bare burdens, with those that laded, every one with one of his hands wrought in the work, and with the other hand held a weapon .

Ezekiel 21:16 Go thee one way or other, either on the right hand, or on the left, whithersoever thy face is set

Out of sight, out of mind.

A reference to quickly forgetting someone or something not recently seen.

Psalm 31:12 I am forgotten as a dead man out of mind: I am like a broken vessel.

Out of the mouths of babes.

Thoughts or words that come from small children. Often used to reference blunt or pointed words, containing mature wisdom, that is spoken by the young.

Psalm 8:2 Out of the mouth of babes and sucklings hast thou ordained strength because of thine enemies, that thou mightest still the enemy and the avenger.

Matthew 21:16 And said unto him, Hearest thou what these say? And Jesus saith unto them, Yea; have ye never read, Out of the mouth of babes and sucklings thou hast perfected praise?

People in glass houses shouldn't throw stones.

One should not point out the faults and sins of others when they commit the same, for when a stone is thrown at their "house" it will break and reveal their sin.

John 8:7 ...He that is without sin among you, let him first cast a stone at her.

Physician, heal thyself.

An exhortation to take action to correct (heal) one's own faults, sins and mistakes, rather than pointing out the faults, etc. of others.

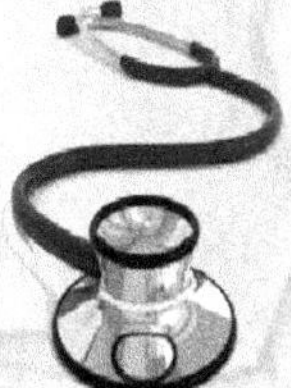

Luke 4:23 And he said unto them, Ye will surely say unto me this proverb, Physician, heal thyself: whatsoever we have heard done in Capernaum, do also here in thy country.

Pride comes before a fall.

Being self-centered and ego-driven will lead to ruin.

Proverbs 16:18 Pride goeth before destruction, and an haughty spirit before a fall.

Put your house in order.

Get your business or personal affairs organized. This is sometimes used in reference to impending death.

2 Kings 20:1 In those days was Hezekiah sick unto death. And the prophet Isaiah the son of Amoz came to him, and said unto him, Thus saith the LORD, Set thine house in order; for thou shalt die, and not live.

Isaiah 38:1 In those days was Hezekiah sick unto death. And Isaiah the prophet the son of Amoz came unto him, and said unto him, Thus saith the LORD, Set thine house in order: for thou shalt die, and not live.

Red sky in morning, sailors take warning; Red sky at night, sailors' delight.

This has a literal meaning of looking at the sky to discern impending weather.

Matthew 16:2-3 He answered and said unto them, When it is evening, ye say, It will be fair weather: for the sky is red. And in the morning, It will be foul weather to day: for the sky is red and lowering

Raising Cain.

This phrase is used in reference to causing great trouble, creating chaos, promoting extreme distress, etc. It derives from the book of Genesis, when Cain became jealous of his brother Abel and killed him.

Genesis 4:8 And Cain talked with Abel his brother: and it came to pass, when they were in the field, that Cain rose up against Abel his brother, and slew him.

Rise and shine.

This means to wake up (just as the sun rises) and be happy (let the light in your life shine).

Isaiah 60:1 Arise, shine; for thy light is come, and the glory of the LORD is risen upon thee.

Safe and sound.

Free from physical or mental harm.

Luke 15:27 And he said unto him, Thy brother is come; and

thy father hath killed the fatted calf, because he hath received him safe and sound.

Seeing eye to eye.

A reference to agreement with another or others. Avoiding eye contact can be an indicator of disagreement or lack of trust or acceptance.

Isaiah 52:8 Thy watchmen shall lift up the voice; with the voice together shall they sing: for they shall see eye to eye, when the LORD shall bring again Zion.

Seek and you shall find.

This phrase is used as an optimistic exhort to encourage someone to look, or continue looking, until they find what they are looking for.

Matthew 7:7 Ask, and it shall be given you; seek, and ye shall find; knock, and it shall be opened unto you:

Separate the wheat from the chaff.

To distinguish what is useful or valuable from what is not.

In the biblical times the chaff was separated by a process called winnowing. The wheat was tossed into the air and the chaff would be carried away by the wind, while the wheat would fall to the floor.

Jeremiah 23:28 The prophet that hath a dream, let him tell a dream; and he that hath my word, let him speak my word faithfully. What is the chaff to the wheat? saith the LORD.

Matthew 3:12 Whose fan is in his hand, and he will thoroughly purge his floor, and gather his wheat into the garner; but he will burn up the chaff with unquenchable fire.

Shake the dust from your feet.

Depart indignantly or depart without looking back.

Matthew 10:14 If anyone will not welcome you or listen to your words, shake the dust off your feet when you leave that home or town.

Mark 6:11 And whosoever shall not receive you, nor hear you, when ye depart thence, shake off the dust under your feet for a testimony against them.

Luke 9:5 And whoever will not receive you, when you go out of that city, shake off the very dust from your feet as a testimony against them."

Acts 13:51 But they shook off the dust of their feet against them and came unto Iconium.

Sharper than a two-edged sword.

Sharper than sharp. The sharpest, most lethal of weapons.

Psalm 149:6 Let the high praises of God be in their mouth, and a twoedged sword in their hand;

Proverbs 5:4 But her end is bitter as wormwood, sharp as a twoedged sword.

Hebrews 4:12 For the word of God is quick, and powerful, and sharper than any twoedged sword, piercing even to the dividing asunder of soul and spirit, and of the joints and marrow, and is a discerner of the thoughts and intents of the heart.

Revelation 1:16 And he had in his right hand seven stars: and out of his mouth went a sharp twoedged sword: and his countenance was as the sun shineth in his strength.

Revelation 2:12 And to the angel of the church in Pergamos write; These things saith he which hath the sharp sword with two edges

Shout it from the rooftop.

Indicates a desire to proclaim something loudly and widely. During biblical times this was an effective way to reach a large audience of people.

Matthew 10:27 What I tell you in darkness, that speak ye in light: and what ye hear in the ear, that preach ye upon the housetops.

Sign of the Times.

Something that signifies the current times.

Matthew 16:3 And in the morning, It will be foul weather to day: for the sky is red and lowring. O ye hypocrites, ye can discern, the face of the sky; but can ye not discern the signs of the times?

Sinking in the mire (or stuck in the mire)

Mire is a swampy, muddy, dirty piece of ground. This means to be immersed in a messy or difficult situation.

Jeremiah 38:6 Then took they Jeremiah, and cast him into the dungeon of Malchiah the son of Hammelech, that was in the court of the prison: and they let down Jeremiah with cords. And in the dungeon there was no water, but mire: so Jeremiah sunk in the mire.

Smooth as butter or slick like butter.

(This has evolved over time into "buttering someone up.")

This is used in reference to someone's words of excessive flattery, kindness or agreement, often with insincerity and ulterior motives behind the words.

Psalm 55:21 The words of his mouth were smoother than butter, but war was in his heart: his words were softer than oil, yet were they drawn swords.

Spare the rod and spoil the child.

This teaches that children need to understand wrongdoing and that often requires some form of chastisement.

Proverbs 13:24 He that spareth his rod hateth his son: but he that loveth him chasteneth him betimes [promptly].

Proverbs 29:15 The rod and reproof give wisdom: but a child left to himself bringeth his mother to shame.

This phrase is sometimes misused to justify that excessive punishment is necessary for well-behaved children. The verses in Proverbs indicate that the rod was intended for correction and guidance, leading to maturity, not for physical control over another person.

Stay on the straight and narrow.

Follow a conventional or law-abiding course.

Matthew 7:13-14 Enter ye in at the strait gate: for wide is the gate, and broad is the way, that leadeth to destruction, and many there be which go in thereat: Because strait is the gate, and narrow is the way, which leadeth unto life, and few there be that find it.

Straight from the horse's mouth.

Used in reference to credible or trustworthy information, based upon it coming directly from the source.

Numbers 22:28 Then the LORD opened the donkey's mouth, and she [the donkey] said to Balaam, "What have I done to you to make you beat me these three times?"

Tearing your hair out.

A phrase that conveys exasperation with a situation, or grief regarding circumstances.

Ezra 9:3 And when I heard this thing, I rent my garment and my mantle, and plucked off the hair of my head and of my beard, and sat down astonied

That's forbidden fruit.

A prohibited item.

Genesis 2:16-17 And the LORD God commanded the man, saying, Of every tree of the garden thou mayest freely eat: But of the tree of the knowledge of good and evil, thou shalt not eat of it: for in the day that thou eatest thereof thou shalt surely die.

The blind leading the blind.

Uninformed or incompetent people, who lead others who are similarly incapable.

Luke 6:39 And he spake a parable unto them, Can the blind lead the blind? shall they not both fall into the ditch?

The fruit of your loins.

The children that one has conceived.

Genesis 35:11 And God said unto him, I am God Almighty: be fruitful and multiply; a nation and a company of nations shall be of thee, and kings shall come out of thy loins;

The heart (or root) of the matter.

The beginning or the essential part of something.

Daniel 7:28 Hitherto is the end of the matter. As for me Daniel, my cogitations much troubled me, and my countenance changed in me: but I kept the matter in my heart.

Job 19:28 But ye should say, Why persecute we him, seeing the root of the matter is found in me?

The Land of Nod.

To "go off to the Land of Nod" or to be "in the Land of Nod" refers to being in a place of sleep, separated from those who are awake. In the Bible the Land of Nod was not a place of sleep, but of exile or separation. In reference to sleep, this phrase is often shortened to "Nod off."

Genesis 4:16 And Cain went out from the presence of the LORD, and dwelt in the land of Nod, on the east of Eden.

The left hand doesn't know what the right hand is doing.

Little or no communication, resulting in lack of knowledge.

Matthew 6:3-4 But when you give to the needy, do not let your left hand know what your right hand is doing, so that your giving may be in secret. Then your Father, who sees what is done in secret, will reward you.

The letter of the law.

This means to obey the literal interpretation of the words (the "letter"), but not necessarily the intent or meaning that the law represents.

2 Corinthians 3:6 Who also hath made us able ministers of the new testament; not of the letter, but of the spirit: for the letter killeth, but the spirit giveth life.

The long arm of the law.

The power or authority of the law.

Deuteronomy 26:8 And the LORD brought us forth out of Egypt with a mighty hand, and with an outstretched arm, and with great terribleness, and with signs, and with wonders:

Jeremiah 27:5 I have made the earth, the man and the beast that are upon the ground, by my great power and by my out-stretched arm...

The patience of Job.

This implies having perseverance and forbearance in the most difficult of times or circumstances.

Job endured great suffering, but persevered by faith in God. So also did all the prophets and those who served God. When we read of their sufferings it helps us to see our prob lems with a new perspective and focus our hope in God.

James 5:10-11 Take, my brethren, the prophets, who have spoken in the name of the Lord, for an example of suffering affliction, and of patience. Behold, we count them happy which endure. Ye have heard of the patience of Job, and have seen the end of the Lord; that the Lord is very pitiful, and of tender mercy.

The powers that be.

A reference to those in authority or power.

Romans 13:1 Let every soul be subject unto the higher powers. For there is no power but of God: the powers that be are ordained of God.

The prodigal returns.

Said of someone who has been gone or missing for a long time. From the biblical teaching of the son who left home, taking his inheritance and squandering it. He returned home to be welcomed by his father.

Luke 15:12-13 And the younger of them said to his father, Father, give me the portion of goods that falleth to me. And he divided unto them his living. And not many days after the younger son gathered all together, and took his journey into a far country, and there wasted his substance with riotous living.

Luke 15:20 And he arose, and came to his father.

The Spirit is willing but the flesh is weak.

What one desires can be overtaken by lack of strength, energy or determination; virtuous desires can be overtaken by sins of the flesh/worldly desires.

Matthew 26:41 Watch and pray, that ye enter not into temptation: the spirit indeed is willing, but the flesh is weak.

The writing is on the wall.

Infers that the subject matter is obvious. Usually a reference to impending doom or danger that is certain to occur.

Daniel 5:5 In the same hour came forth fingers of a man's hand, and wrote over against the candlestick upon the plaster of the wall of the king's palace: and the king saw the part of the hand that wrote.

Daniel 5:24 Then was the part of the hand sent from him; and this writing was written.

There is nothing new under the sun.

Everything has already been seen, done, heard, spoken, experienced, etc. This phrase comes from the book of Ecclesiastes, which was written about 3,000 years ago.

Ecclesiastes 1:9 The thing that hath been, it is that which shall be; and that which is done is that which shall be done: and there is no new thing under the sun.

This too shall pass.

Everything will come to an end eventually.

Matthew 24:6 And ye shall hear of wars and rumours of wars: see that ye be not troubled: for all these things must come to pass, but the end is not yet.

Thorn in the flesh.

An irritant that is persistent and annoying to the point of ongoing awareness.

2 Corinthians 12:7 And lest I should be exalted above measure through the abundance of the revelations, there was given to me a thorn in the flesh, the messenger of Satan to buffet me, lest I should be exalted above measure.

To the four corners of the earth.

Far reaching; all encompassing; to every part of the earth.

Isaiah 11:12 And he shall set up an ensign for the nations, and shall assemble the outcasts of Israel, and gather together the dispersed of Judah from the four corners of the earth.

Revelation 7:1 And after these things I saw four angels standing on the four corners of the earth, holding the four winds of the earth, that the wind should not blow on the earth, nor on the sea, nor on any tree.

Turn the other cheek.

To not retaliate. Usually used to refer to not responding to a violent act in like manner.

Matthew 5:39 But I say unto you, That ye resist not evil: but whosoever shall smite thee on thy right cheek, turn to him the other also.

Two heads are better than one.

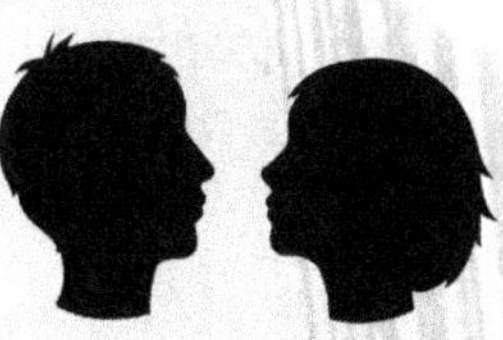

Two minds, or two perspectives and understandings, are beneficial in solving or dealing with a problem.

Ecclesiastes 4:9 Two are better than one; because they have a good reward for their labour.

United we stand, divided we fall.

(Similar to A House Divide)

Division in a united group will cause the group to fail in its purpose and its mission.

Matthew 12:25 Jesus knew their thoughts, and said unto them, Every kingdom divided against itself is brought to desolation; and every city or house divided against itself shall not stand:

Luke 11:17 But he, knowing their thoughts, said unto them, Every kingdom divided against itself is brought to desolation; and a house divided against a house falleth.

Weighed and found wanting.

This phrase is a reference to a measurement or assessment having been taken and the result being less than what was expected or required.

Daniel 5:24-28 Then was the part of the hand sent from him; and this writing was written. And this is the writing that was written, MENE, MENE, TEKEL, UPHARSIN. This is the interpretation of the thing: MENE; God hath numbered thy king-

dom, and finished it. TEKEL; Thou art ***weighed*** *in the balances, and art* ***found wanting****. PERES; Thy kingdom is divided, and given to the Medes and Persians.*

Woe is me.

An expression of sadness, grief or distress.

Psalm 120:5 Woe is me, that I sojourn in Mesech, that I dwell in the tents of Kedar!

Isaiah 6:5 Then said I, Woe is me! for I am undone; because I am a man of unclean lips, and I dwell in the midst of a people of unclean lips: for mine eyes have seen the King, the LORD of hosts.

Written in stone.

Permanently written. Something that cannot be erased. God wrote the Law on tablets of stone and gave them to Moses. Jesus will write the names of overcomers in a stone.

Exodus 31:18 And he gave unto Moses, when he had made an end of communing with him upon mount Sinai, two tables of testimony, tables of stone, written with the finger of God.

Revelation 2:17 He that hath an ear, let him hear what the Spirit saith unto the churches; To him that overcometh will I give to eat of the hidden manna, and will give him a white stone, and in the stone a new name written, which no man knoweth saving he that receiveth it.

Yada, yada, yada.

The final phrase is one that was popularized in the late 1990s. It was used repeatedly during conversations in the 1997 *Seinfeld* TV episode titled "The Yada Yada." This phrase has come to mean "and so on and so forth" -- but it also has a more literal meaning.

It is used primarily in informal conversation to eliminate undesirable or insignificant details, thereby replacing portions of a story or explanation. Because it is assumed that the listener is aware of the information omitted, the phrase implies "you know what I'm talking about."

Most people who use this phrase have no idea of its biblical origin. Yada is the Hebrew word that means "to know," so this phrase can easily be understood to mean "you know, you know, you know."

Although the repetitive, three-times use of the word yada is not found in the Bible to replace words or portions of text, it is included in this book of common sayings as a reminder of the influence the Hebrew language has on our everyday conversations.

Some biblical examples of the use of the word "yada" include the following (NKJV, all emphasis and bracketed information added):

Exodus 29:46 "And they shall ***know*** *[yada] that I am the LORD their God, who brought them up out of the land of Egypt, that I may dwell among them. I am the LORD their God.*

Job 9:2 "Truly I ***know*** *[yada] it is so, But how can a man be righteous before God?*

Psalm 46:10 Be still, and **know** *[yada] that I am God; I will be exalted among the nations, I will be exalted in the earth!*

Habakkuk 2:14 For the earth will be filled With the **knowledge** *[yada] of the glory of the LORD, As the waters cover the sea.*

The God of all creation knows you!

Exodus 33:17 So the LORD said to Moses, "I will also do this thing that you have spoken; for you have found grace in My sight, and I **know** *[yada] you by name."*

Psalm 37:18 The LORD **knows** *[yada] the days of the upright, And their inheritance shall be forever.*

Psalm 139:1-2 O LORD, You have searched me and **known** *[yada] me. You* **know** *[yada] my sitting down and my rising up; You understand my thought afar off.*

Jeremiah 1:5 "Before I formed you in the womb I **knew** *[yada] you...*

The big question is: Do you know Him?

Ecclesiastes 3:14 I **know** *[yada] that whatever God does, It shall be forever.*

Ecclesiastes 7:25 I applied my heart to **know** *[yada], To search and seek out wisdom and the reason of things...*

Psalm 9:10 And those who **know** *[yada] Your name will put their trust in You; For You, LORD, have not forsaken those who seek You.*

Psalm 39:4 "LORD, make me to **know** *[yada] my end, And what is the measure of my days, That I may* **know** *[yada] how frail I am.*

He knows you!

Psalm 44:21 Would not God search this out? For He ***knows*** *[yada] the secrets of the heart.*

Psalm 69:5 O God, You ***know*** *[yada] my foolishness; And my sins are not hidden from You.*

Do you know Him?

Psalm 135:5 For I ***know*** *[yada] that the LORD is great, And our Lord is above all gods.*

Jeremiah 9:23-24 Thus says the LORD: "Let not the wise man glory in his wisdom, Let not the mighty man glory in his might, Nor let the rich man glory in his riches; But ***let him who glories glory in this, That he understands and knows*** *[yada]* ***Me****, That I am the LORD, exercising lovingkindness, judgment, and righteousness in the earth. For in these I delight," says the LORD.*

In John 14:4, 6 Jesus said,

*"...**the way you know**...*

I am the way, the truth, and the life.

No one comes to the Father except through Me."

A Three Strand Cord

A three strand cord is strong and "not quickly broken" (Ecclesiastes 4:12). A three strand cord—black, gold and red—can be used to understand the gospel message:

A black strand reminds us of our sin:
There is none righteous; all have sinned and fall short of the glory of God. (Romans 3:10, 23)

A gold strand reminds us of the love of God:
For God so loved the world, that he gave his only begotten Son, that whosoever believeth in him should not perish, but have everlasting life. (John 3:16)

A red strand reminds us of Christ's blood, shed for our sins:
Without shedding of blood there is no remission [of sin]; Christ died for our sins...was buried...was raised on the third day (Hebrews 9:22, 1 Corinthians 15:3-4)

Remember the mighty strength of the Triune God and His three-fold assurance.

1) He promises forgiveness and salvation to all who turn from their sins and trust in the life, death, burial and resurrection of the Lord Jesus Christ.

2) He is Faithful and True (Romans 19:11), and

3) He gives life to all who come to Him in faith. His gift is freely given and it is forever secure.

"And I give them eternal life, and they shall never perish; neither shall anyone snatch them out of My hand. My Father, who has given them to Me, is greater than all; and no one is able to snatch them out of My Father's hand. I and My Father are one."

John 10:28-30 (NKJV)

If you don't know Jesus Christ, repent of your sins today. Confess them, and ask Jesus for forgiveness. Turn from your sins and turn to Jesus. Trust that He loves you and that He paid the penalty for your sins.

We are all only one heartbeat away from taking our last breath and stepping into eternity. Jesus promises that He has prepared a place for all who belong to Him.

"Let not your heart be troubled; you believe in God, believe also in Me. In My Father's house are many mansions; if it were not so, I would have told you. I go to prepare a place for you. And if I go and prepare a place for you, I will come again and receive you to Myself; that where I am, there you may be also. And where I go you know, and the way you know." Jesus said..."I am the way, the truth, and the life. No one comes to the Father except through Me. John 14:1-4,6 (NKJV)

Take a few minutes and search your heart. Think about the God of the universe, who loves you and came to earth to seek and save sinners. He lived the life we cannot live and He died the death that we should die; and He offers eternal life to all who come to Him in faith.

If your heart desires to know Jesus, pray something like this: *Lord Jesus, I know that I have sinned and I am not worthy of your forgiveness. Your Word, the Bible, tells me that You died to forgive my sins; and You promise that if I turn from my sins and turn to You, then you will grant me forgiveness. I desire to know You, and I trust in Your finished work on the cross to pay for my sins. I ask that you forgive my sins and grant me eternal life. Please save me; and help me to live my life in a way that honors You. In Jesus' name I pray. Amen.*

If you prayed that prayer, please let us know by emailing **hope@reasonsforhopeJesus.com.** We would like to send you information that will help you grow in faith. If you have questions, please email us at **hope@reasonsforhopeJesus.**

Who said that? Now you know. Isn't it amazing that the words of Holy Scripture, which date back many thousands of years, are so frequently used in everyday conversation?

The next time you hear one of these sayings, remember where it came from and who said it! Share your knowledge with someone today and use these common, everyday sayings to open a door for a spiritual conversation.

Choose your words wisely.

Share your faith often.

Tell someone today about the saving grace of Jesus Christ!

All scripture is given by inspiration of God, and is profitable for doctrine, for reproof, for correction, for instruction in righteousness: That the man of God may be perfect, thoroughly furnished unto all good works.

(2 Timothy 3:16-17)

Favorite Sayings

What are some of your favorite sayings? Can you find them in the Bible?

Think about some everyday sayings that you hear or use. Record them in the space below, and then search your Bible to determine if they have biblical origins. Have fun!

If you find some, please share them with us by emailing to hope@reasonsforhopeJesus.com

Scripture Index

Books & Resources from this Author

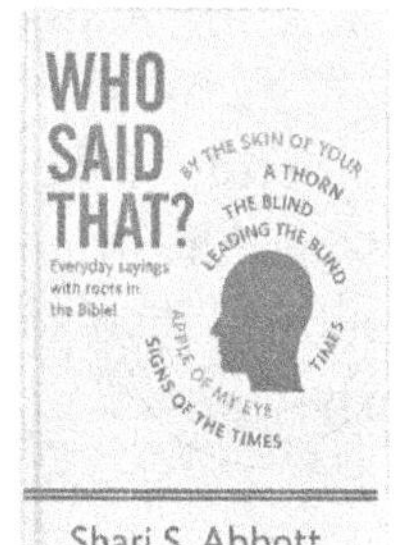

Who Said That? Common Everyday Sayings
This is a great book to give to unbelievers. It's simply a look at everyday sayings originating from God's Word. At the end of the book is a gospel presentation.

A Room with a View of Eternity—The Last Will & Testament of the Lord Jesus Christ
Take a seat at the Master's table. Learn about the Lord's final words to His faithful disciples (John 13-17), and the riches He gives to all who are His. This book will bless and encourage you, provide you with hope, and help you live in the joy of your salvation.

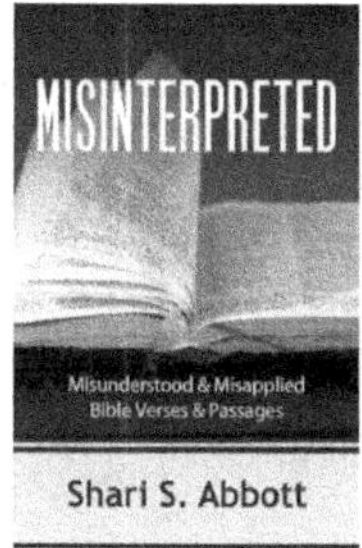

MISINTERPRETED - Misunderstood & Misapplied Bible Verses & Passages—Sometimes Scripture is wrongly taught with an intention to deceive, but most often it is unintentional. As Christians, we must be diligent in discerning truth —God's truth from His Word.

Got Questions? We have Reasons for Hope
Reasons Books 1, 2, 3 & 4

Real questions from real people. Each book has 30 questions and 30 answers with reasons for hope.

Why the Butterfly? Rightly Remembering Jesus—This book isn't about butterflies. . .it's all about Jesus! Discover how rightly remembering will establish your heart, anchor your soul, and transform your mind. A quick read that will give you a heavenly perspective on this journey we call life!

Remember Me - A Course About Rightly Remembering
Seven video study sessions that teach rightly remembering and will ignite in you a desire to filter everything you think, say and do through the hope that is found in Jesus Christ. Learn how *rightly remembering* will establish your heart, anchor your soul, and transform your mind.

Fun with Shuns Learn the key doctrines of the Christian faith by understanding the many words in the Bible that end in "-tion". The study includes five short videos. If you can't fully explain why you believe what you believe, then you need this study. DVD and book for group or individual study.

Hear, See, Speak No Evil—Plus a Fourth Monkey
The three little monkeys, with their proverbial quip, "Hear No Evil, See No Evil, and Speak No Evil," date back as far as 17th century. What biblical lessons do these monkeys offer? And what about the newest warning. . .post no evil?

How to Witness to Jehovah's Witnesses, Apologetics Answers & Verses Get prepared to defend what you believe and be able to present biblical truth the next time a Jehovah's Witness comes to your door. Don't be out-witnessed by a Jehovah's Witness.

Quotable Quotes - Words Worth Remembering — s a treasury of timeless wisdom from Christian voices across the ages. Carefully chosen quotations are paired with Scripture references to encourage you to delve deeper into the biblical truths that relate to the insightful quotes..

Forty Names of Jesus for Forty Days of Lent — A daily devotional companion inviting you to slow down, open God's Word, and fix your heart on Jesus by reflecting on one of His many names and titles. Allow the Holy Spirit to deepen your love for "The Risen Christ," your Shepherd, Savior, and King.

Rightly Dividing the Word of Truth —With simple explanations and Scripture-centered teaching, you'll discover how a right understanding of Scripture brings clarity instead of confusion, confidence instead of doubt, and joy as you see how every part of the Bible fits together in God's perfect plan. This is your invitation to become a faithful workman—*rightly dividing the Word of Truth.*

Visit www.reasonsforhopeJesus.com/store

This hope we have as an anchor for the soul, both sure and steadfast. (Hebrews 6:19)

Helping Christians to know Jesus better, by

Offering biblical answers and reasoning from God's Word, and

Promoting the benefits and joys of spending time with God in prayer and in reading and studying His Word, which leads to

Enjoying God, finding rest in Jesus, and living to honor Him and serve others.

Get *equipped* with KNOWLEDGE!

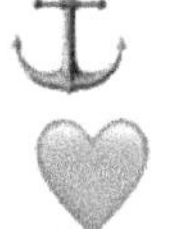
Be *encouraged* in HOPE!

Live *empowered* with LOVE!

About Reasons for Hope* Jesus

Our ministry exists to glorify God by equipping Christians with biblical knowledge, understanding, and wisdom. Knowing and trusting God and growing in understanding of His will and ways will change our world. Jesus is the Reason this Ministry Exists, but YOU make it possible!

If Reasons for Hope* Jesus has blessed you, please consider supporting our ministry. Your goodwill and generosity makes possible our mission to equip, encourage, and empower the body of Christ and reach the lost with the gospel of saving grace. www.reasonsforhopeJesus.com/donate.

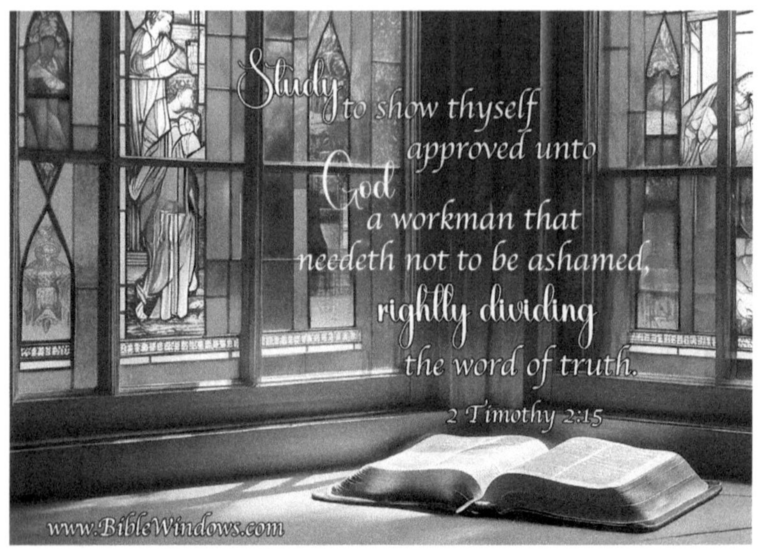

Visit www.BibleWindows.com
for all our song videos and
Bible teachings videos

Questions?

Email us at questions@reasonsforhopeJesus.com

Contact Us

Email us at hope@reasonsforhopeJesus.com

Connect With Us

www.reasonsforhopeJesus.com

www.biblewindows.com

Facebook: www.facebook.com/reasonsforhopeJesus/

Twitter: www.twitter.com/reasons4hope

YouTube: www.youtube.com/reasonsforhopeJesus

Visit the Store

www.reasonsforhopeJesus.com/store

Sign Up

At www.reasonsforhopeJesus.com for apologetics teachings and biblical encouragement with true hope and real joy.

May the God of hope fill you with all joy and peace in believing, that you may abound in hope by the power of the Holy Spirit. Romans 15:13

Have Hope!

Now hope does not disappoint, because the love of God has been poured out in our hearts by the Holy Spirit who was given to us.

—Romans 5:5

Be Bold!

Therefore, since we have such hope, we use great boldness of speech;

—2 Corinthians 3:12

[Praying] for me, that utterance may be given to me, that I may open my mouth boldly to make known the mystery of the gospel, for which I am an ambassador in chains; that in it I may speak boldly, as I ought to speak.

—Ephesians 6:19-20

www.ingramcontent.com/pod-product-compliance
Lightning Source LLC
LaVergne TN
LVHW011047110826
845149LV00015B/3397